know your pet

GUINEA PIGS

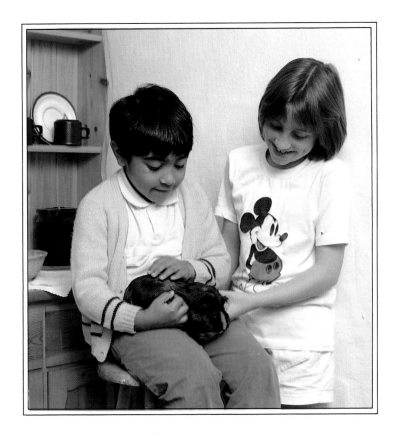

Anna and Michael Sproule

The Bookwright Press
New York · 1989

Know Your Pet

Cats	Rabbits
Dogs	Hamsters
Ponies	Aquarium Fish
Gerbils	Guinea Pigs
Parakeets	Mice and Rats

First published in the
United States in 1989 by
The Bookwright Press
387 Park Avenue South
New York, NY 10016

First published in 1989 by
Wayland (Publishers) Limited,
61 Western Road, Hove,
East Sussex, BN3 1JD, England.

© BLA Publishing Limited 1989

Library of Congress Cataloging-in-Publication Data

Guinea pigs/by Anna and Michael Sproule
    p.   cm. — (Know your pet)
Bibliography: p.
Includes index.
Summary: Describes the physical characteristics,
habits, and natural environment of guinea pigs and
gives instructions on how to care for them as pets.
  ISBN 0-531-18265-7
  1. Guinea pigs as pets — Juvenile literature.
[1. Guinea pigs. 2.Pets.] I. Sproule, Michael. II. Title.
III. Series.
SF459.G9S67 1989
636'.93234—dc 19
                     88-26221
                     CIP
                     AC

Photographic credits

t = top, b = bottom, l = left, r = right

cover: Trevor Hill

All photographs by Trevor Hill except:
10 Bruce Coleman Limited

The photographer and the publishers would like to
thank Mike and Wendy Penny, The Mid-Sussex
Cavy Club and the families and their guinea pigs
who participated in the photography for this book.

Designed and produced by BLA Publishing
Limited, East Grinstead, Sussex, England.

A member of the Ling Kee Group
LONDON · HONG KONG · TAIPEI · SINGAPORE · NEW YORK

Editorial planning by Jollands Editions
Illustrations by Graham Allen/Linden Artists; Steve
Lings/Linden Artists and Jane Pickering/
Linden Artists
Printed in Italy

**Cover: You have only to look at the picture
on the cover of this book to realize
why guinea pigs are so popular as
pets. They are clean, cuddly and
attractive in appearance. They greet
you with a whole range of friendly
noises which is their way of
expressing their feelings.**

**Title page: Guinea pigs are by nature timid,
but they soon become very
tame. If you are nearby to watch
them, you can let your friends
handle your pet, but they must
be very quiet and gentle.**

Contents

Note to the Reader

In this book there are some words in the text that are printed in **bold** type. This shows that the word is listed in the glossary on page 44. The glossary gives a brief explanation of words that may be new to you.

Introduction

Before you decide to keep a pet, you need to ask yourself some questions. Is there room at your home to keep it? Will you have the time to care for it? Does everyone in your family think that having a pet in the home is a good idea?

If you want to keep guinea pigs, you will need a garden shed, or a safe, sheltered yard for the hutch and run. If you live where it gets as cold as 10 degrees below freezing, you will also need some indoor shelter. Looking after your pets will take only a short time each day. But you must spend the time *every* day, and have someone else take over when you are away. Healthy guinea pigs live for five years or more and need care throughout their lives.

Guinea pigs as pets

Guinea pigs are easy to tame and enjoy being handled by their owners. They soon learn to come forward for their food at meal times, and to recognize voices. They are **rodents**, but unlike some other gnawing animals they do not climb or **burrow**. They are not likely to try to escape, but their home must be strong and safe to keep other animals from getting in.

▲ A fully grown guinea pig weighs about 900 g (2 lb). You must hold it securely, but not too tightly, as a guinea pig's bones are very small and fragile.

◄ If you would like to own a pet that is a bit different, you could choose a rough-haired guinea pig. But you will have to groom rough-haired and long-haired breeds every day, or their coats will soon become matted and dirty.

▲ Guinea pigs in the wild live in grasslands. It helps to keep them in good condition if you can put your pets out on the grass from time to time. The outdoor run must be in a position where they get shade from the sun.

Once you have bought a hutch and a run guinea pigs cost very little to keep, but you will need enough money to buy food and fresh hay for bedding for as long as they remain yours to care for.

Needs and behavior

It is important to give your guinea pigs an outdoor run where they can get some **exercise**. In the wild, guinea pigs live in family groups, and yours will be happier if you keep two or more. They should be of the same sex, and you should buy them at the same time so that they get used to each other while they are young. If the hutch and run are large enough, guinea pigs can be kept with a rabbit.

Guinea pigs are nervous animals. You should keep them in a place where they will not be scared by cats or dogs, or by sudden loud noises nearby.

About guinea pigs

Guinea pigs come from South America. They are rodents, and belong to the same animal order as hamsters, rats, mice and gerbils.

Guinea pigs are in a group of rodents called **cavies**. There are about twenty **species** of cavies in South America. Some, like the Bolivian cavies, live high up in the Andes mountains. They live in burrows or make nests among rocks. Other guinea pigs are lowland animals living on grasslands at the foot of mountains. They make their homes in the open air, forming hollow nests in the long grass.

Life in the wild

Guinea pigs live in **colonies** or family groups, and this is why it is best to keep two as pets. They are **vegetarians**, living on seeds and dried grass.

Like other small animals that live in the open, guinea pigs are likely to be attacked by larger, meat-eating enemies at any time. This explains why they are rather timid and easily frightened, even when they are kept in safety as pets. They cannot move quickly, and if they are frightened their **instinct** is to hide. As pets, they like to have a dark, quiet place where they can go to feel safe.

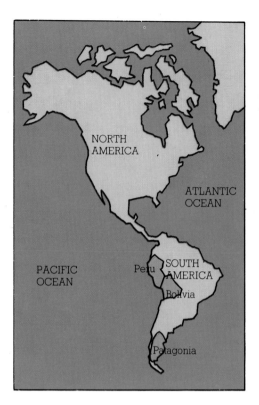

▲ Wild guinea pigs, or cavies as they are also called, come from the grasslands of Peru, Bolivia and Patagonia in South America. There are about twenty different species. They are social animals, living in colonies or in family groups.

◀ This photo shows a group of Patagonian cavies in their natural habitat. The coat of a wild guinea pig is of a grayish, pepper and salt appearance, due to the fact that the hairs are tipped with black.

10

▼ The pictures below show a number of guinea pig varieties. The Abyssinian is rough-haired, the Peruvian long-haired and the others are smooth-haired.

smooth-haired

Young animals born in the open, like guinea pigs and hares, must be able to look after themselves soon after they are born. They have no burrows where they can stay warm and safe until they are ready to venture outside. Young guinea pigs are born with teeth, and with their eyes already open. Only two days after they are born in the wild, they start to eat the same food as their parents.

Guinea pigs in the wild spend most of the day searching for food. Pet guinea pigs do not need to search, but they still have the instinct to do so. This instinct to find out all they can about the world around them is one of the things that makes them such interesting pets.

Himalayan

Abyssinian

Peruvian

Dutch

Tortoiseshell

What is a guinea pig?

About 450 years ago, Spain sent an army to conquer Central and South America. Soon afterward, Spanish ships began to carry cargoes between South American and Europe, and sailors brought guinea pigs back with them. Soon, people in Europe began to keep and breed guinea pigs as pets. They first arrived in Britain around 1750.

Why "guinea pigs"?

Guinea pigs are not related to farmyard pigs and look nothing like them. There are many ideas about how they got their name. One reason may be that the Indians who lived in South America before the Spanish came bred guinea pigs for meat, and this reminded the Spanish of pork. Some people say that the guinea pig's squeak is rather like that of a small pig.

▼ A male and female breeding pair. The adult male, called a boar, is generally larger, weighing about 1 kg (2 lb). The female, called a sow weighs a few ounces less. In this picture the ginger guinea pig is the male.

▲ Newborn guinea pigs are fully developed at birth. They have full coats, their eyes are open and they are ready to take solid food within a day or two of birth.

▼ The cheek teeth of a guinea pig, as well as the front teeth, go on growing and have to be worn down by gnawing. The front paws have four toes, the hind paws only three toes.

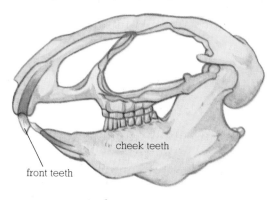

cheek teeth

front teeth

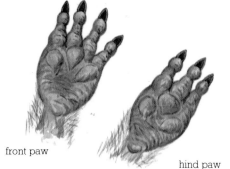

front paw

hind paw

As for the "guinea" part of their name, it may be that the sailors who first brought them back to Spain sailed from Guiana on the coast of South America. Another explanation could be that the golden-brown color of some guinea pigs reminded people of a golden guinea coin. Perhaps the Portuguese word *guiné* is a clue. It means "a far away land."

No one is sure of the truth, so you can choose any explanation you like. Some people prefer to use the scientific name "cavy." But whether you call your pet a cavy or a guinea pig, the male is called a **boar** and the female a **sow**.

Rodents

Like all rodents, guinea pigs nibble at their food with their sharp front teeth. Unlike human teeth, these continue to grow all through the guinea pig's life and are worn down by gnawing and nibbling. Even if a tooth breaks, it will go on growing. Behind the front teeth there is another set of teeth, which the guinea pig uses to grind its food before swallowing.

Guinea pigs are active in the daytime and sleep at night. When they are awake they spend a great deal of time eating, but they seldom eat more than they need.

Living quarters

Before you buy your guinea pigs you will need a hutch, but first you must decide where it is to go. Guinea pigs can be kept outside except during very cold weather. Where the temperature drops to −6°C (20°F), you will need to put the hutch in a heated garage or an enclosed porch, or even the basement.

The indoor hutch

A hutch for two guinea pigs should be at least 120 cm (4 ft) long, 60 cm (2 ft) wide and 50 cm (20 in) high. Many of those sold in pet shops are too small. It is a good idea to see some rabbit hutches which are larger. Make sure that the hutch you buy will fit into the space where it is to go.

The hutch should have two "rooms," with a door at the front of each. The "bedroom" has solid wooden walls, with a hole through which a guinea pig can go in and out. It is useful if there is a sliding door so that you can shut off

▼ The picture shows two different types of indoor hutches. The larger of the two is the type you should use if you do not have a lawn of grass for an outdoor run. The hutch should be on "legs" so that it will stand clear of the ground.

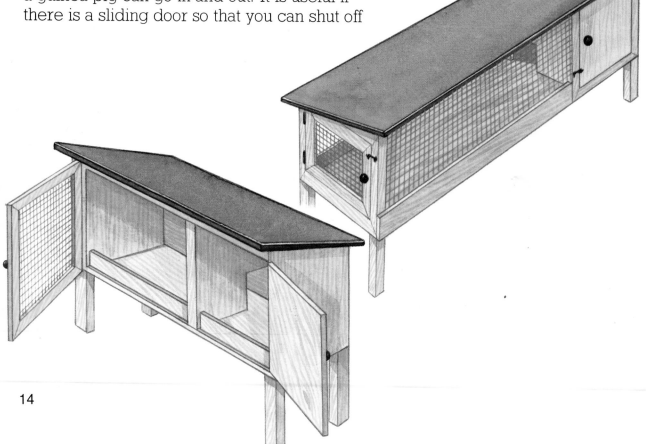

one side while you clean the other. The other "room" should have a wire mesh front door and can also have mesh on the end.

The hutch must stand on legs to keep it away from drafts, and to discourage unwelcome visitors such as cats, dogs and mice.

The outdoor hutch and run

You must be careful where you put an outdoor hutch. It should be away from drafts and rain, but not in direct sunlight. The hutch can be similar to an indoor one, but make sure that rain cannot get in.

Whether you keep the hutch indoors or outside, it will help your pet's health if it can spend fine days in a larger run. Pet shops sell these, but with help you may be able to make one. The sides are made of wire netting, with a small sleeping area shut off at one end. It can be put out on the grass, and moved to a new place each day.

▼ Your pets will benefit if you can give them an outdoor hutch and run as well as an indoor hutch. In warm weather they can live outdoors. You will need to move the run every few days so that your pets can have fresh grass to eat.

Bedding and equipment

Unlike some other small pets, guinea pigs do not need toys to play with. They amuse themselves by eating and playing in their bedding. By following a few simple rules, it is easy to make the hutch a happy, healthy place for your pets to live in.

Bedding for your pets

The thing that guinea pigs like best is hay. They like eating it, sleeping in it and playing with it. Buy the best hay that you can find, in small amounts so that it is always dry and sweet. When you buy it make sure that it is not made from grass that has been treated with **chemicals**. Never use hay from the roadside. It may have been treated with chemicals or **polluted** by traffic fumes.

In the bottom of the hutch you should put a thick layer of wood shavings. Again, these must come from wood that has not been treated. The shavings sometimes used in packaging are usually good, but do not use sawdust, which can get into a guinea pig's eyes. Cleaning the hutch will be made easier if you lay the wood shavings on a pad of newspaper so that you can lift it all out together.

Equipment

You will need a few things to put in the hutch. The food bowl should be heavy, so that it cannot be knocked over easily. Pet shops sell special feeders that clip onto wire mesh. A drip-feed water bottle should be fixed to the wire, with its spout well above the bedding. Choose a bottle with a metal, not a plastic spout. Nothing made of plastic should be allowed inside the hutch, as guinea pigs will chew it. Sharp pieces of plastic can injure the mouth and, if swallowed, cause a stomach upset.

▼ Give your pets the largest hutch you can afford. Guinea pigs do not need toys to play with, but you should make sure that they always have plenty of fresh hay. They eat it, play in it and use it as nesting material. The food bowl should be heavy so that the guinea pigs cannot knock it over. Keep a small log in the hutch. They will gnaw at the wood to keep their teeth in trim.

Guinea pigs enjoy gnawing, and it will help to keep their front teeth in trim. You can buy gnawing-blocks, but any small log of hard wood will do just as well. Guinea pigs do not always use nesting-boxes to sleep in, but you should provide one in case it is needed.

Choosing your pets

Do not be in too much of a hurry to choose your guinea pigs. Take your time and see as many different ones as you can. If there is a breeder who lives near you, arrange a visit. Look in store windows and the local newspaper for notices about guinea pigs for sale. Never buy a pet just because it is cheap. Look for animals in tip-top condition.

If you know anyone who has kept guinea pigs, it would be a good idea to ask them to come and help you choose.

Buying a pair

Guinea pigs like company so it is nice to have a pair. The two animals should be of the same sex, and should have been reared together. If not, they may fight. It is always best to buy young guinea pigs, between six and eight weeks old.

▶ These children are looking at a new litter of Himalayan guinea pigs. They have smooth coats with light, creamy-colored bodies. They have dark points on ears and feet, like those of Siamese cats.

▼ When you have decided to buy a particular breed of guinea pig, it is a good idea to visit a breeder who will help you to make a choice.

▼ Now is the time to make the final choice. Handle the guinea pig and look carefully at the coat and the condition of the skin.

How to make your choice

It is most important to choose animals that are in good health. At six weeks, they should weigh about 250 g (9 oz), and look plump and well-fed. They should look **cobby** — that is, solid and firm. Their eyes should be bright and they should not blink often. The coat should be **closed**, the guinea pig breeder's word for smooth. There should be no signs of runniness from eyes or nose.

The best sign of good health is the way a guinea pig behaves. Do not choose one that is huddled up and takes little interest in what is going on. A healthy guinea pig is alert and lively. You should be able to tempt it to come to the front of its hutch for a tidbit, or just to smell your finger.

Anyone selling you a guinea pig should let you handle it. This will give you a chance to run your hand lightly over its coat to check for bald patches or dry skin. Hold the guinea pig near to you and listen for noisy breathing. A guinea pig that wheezes is in poor health.

Taking your pets home

Your new pets will want to settle into their new home with as little fuss as possible. Make sure before you collect them that their hutch is ready. There should be plenty of clean, fresh bedding, with food in the bowl and water in the drinking bottle. A good bundle of loose hay will make the new home look interesting. Make sure that all bedding is completely dry.

◀ It is an exciting moment bringing your new pets home for the first time. You may need the traveling box again. Clean it out and store it away for the future in a dry place.

▼ These two young guinea pigs explore their new home. Soon it will be time to give them their first meal. The hutch is supported on bricks instead of legs. This is a good idea. You can raise the height as you want by adding more bricks.

Exploring the home

Your guinea pigs may be nervous and shy at first. It is best to leave them to explore their hutch without interference. Other people in the house may want to come and see the new arrivals, but give the guinea pigs time to settle in first. Take great care to keep dogs and cats out of the way.

The guinea pigs will want to explore their new home, looking into every corner. For them, the most important thing is to decide where they are going to sleep. They will move their bedding around until they have found a place they like. This may be quite different from the place you had planned for them.

Once your pets have settled in and are satisfied that their new home is safe and pleasant to live in, you can let your friends and family come to see them. But remember that guinea pigs are frightened by sudden loud noises, and will not enjoy being handled by a number of strange people.

Daily feeding

It is a good idea to feed your pets at the same time every day. They need one meal a day, but it does not matter what time of day they have it. You can choose a time that is best for you — early evening is best for most people. Then you will have time to clean the food bowl and clear away any spilled food without having to do it in a hurry. You can watch your pets while they enjoy their food. At the same time you can fill the drinking bottle with fresh water and check the state of the bedding.

▼ If the weather is fine you can let your new pets explore their outdoor run. You can buy a run like this one at a pet shop.

Handling guinea pigs

Guinea pigs enjoy being handled by their owners, but it is important to learn how to handle them correctly. A young guinea pig may not have been handled before and will need time to get used to it. Start by picking it up and holding it for a short while, slowly increasing the amount of handling each day. When your pet has found out that being handled is pleasant and not frightening, it will start to enjoy its daily cuddle.

Remember that a guinea pig is a small animal with **fragile** bones. Always hold it lightly, with just enough firmness to keep it safe in your hands. Do not go on handling a guinea pig that tries to squirm out of your grasp. Put it back in its hutch at once.

It is best not to let very young children hold a guinea pig. Instead, let them touch and stroke it while you hold it.

◄ **Always use both hands when cuddling your pet. Support the hind legs with one hand. Hold your pet gently around the shoulders with the other hand.**

► When picking up a guinea pig you must always use both hands to hold it. Do not grasp it too firmly around the neck. It will be uncomfortable and may wriggle out of your grasp.

▼ This is a large guinea pig and it needs to be held securely and firmly. Always remember that a guinea pig can be seriously hurt if it is dropped.

Picking up a guinea pig

Sudden movements frighten guinea pigs. When you pick yours up, move slowly and quietly, and always let it see what you are doing. Approach it from the front on the same level, and never try to pick it up from above or behind.

You will need both hands free. Slide one underneath the animal's **rump** to take the weight of its body, and place the other hand over its shoulders. Once you have it safely, you can arrange your hands so that it sits comfortably on one hand while the other hand goes over the back to hold it steady. Bring your hands into your waist so that your stomach helps to support the guinea pig.

Never pick up a guinea pig by the scruff of its neck, or by putting your hands around its middle. Once you are holding it do not let it flop over the edge of your hand. **Pregnant** sows should be handled as little as possible, and not at all in the last weeks of pregnancy.

Feeding guinea pigs

Guinea pigs are vegetarian. Hay, grain and greens are their basic foods. Rabbit **pellets** from the pet shop are made of hay and grain, and together with fresh greens they are an ideal **diet** for guinea pigs. Or you can feed greens, hay and a homemade mixture of grains.

Guinea pigs are not greedy, and will stop eating when they have had enough. It will probably take you a few days to work out the right amount of food to give your pets. It is better to start by giving too much than too little. If some of the food is left uneaten, provide a little less each time until you get it right. Any uneaten food should be cleared away, not left in the hutch to spoil.

Basic foods

Instead of rabbit pellets, you can give hay and a homemade mixture containing rolled oats, crushed corn and bran. This can be served dry or mixed with a little water to make a

▼ Here is a Beige-based Argenté guinea pig eating its evening meal. You should provide a solid food bowl that cannot be knocked over or spilled.

mash. Your pets will need about an adult handful of this mixture once a day. They will enjoy a few sunflower seeds mixed in. Be sure to give hay and greens as well. For special treats to feed from your hand, try small pieces of bread crust or shelled unsalted peanuts.

Greens

You must always include some greens in the diet. All animals need a chemical called **vitamin C** for good health. Most animals make their own inside their bodies, but guinea pigs — like humans — cannot do this. They need to eat foods that contain vitamin C, and the main source is fresh greens.

Cabbage and cauliflower leaves, lettuce, carrot-tops, slices of apple, carrot or raw potato, and pieces of celery all contain plenty of vitamin C. You can also give some wild plants such as coltsfoot, clover, yarrow, shepherd's purse and dandelion leaves. But do not give them foxglove, buttercups, bulbs or any leaves you are not sure of. Wash all fresh greens every time in case they have had chemicals sprayed on them. Feed greens every day, but in small amounts, because they may give your pets **diarrhea** and upset their stomachs.

dandelion

coltsfoot

yarrow

clover

▲ ▼ Guinea pigs need a varied diet. You can give them leaves of certain wild plants, as shown above, and slices of fruit and vegetables as shown below.

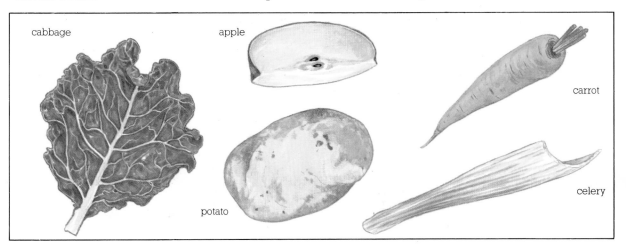

cabbage

apple

carrot

potato

celery

Caring for your pets

Guinea pigs like to have their food at a regular time. You should set aside a few minutes at the same time every day for your pets' mealtime. After a few days your guinea pigs will come forward eager for their food when they see you coming. At the time you give them their meal, provide a handful of fresh, dry hay for them to eat, play with and nest in. This is also the time to empty the drinking bottle and fill it with fresh water.

Handling time

Your pets will soon become tame if you also have a daily "handling time." Give them time to **digest** their food first, and do not let them get overtired by handling them for too long. Be careful not to play favorites. Each guinea pig should have the same amount of care.

▼ Your pet will come forward eagerly when you have a special treat to offer it. If you have two guinea pigs, make sure they both receive the same treats and the same attention.

► Every day you should set aside some time for playing with your guinea pigs and handling them. You can use this time to do a health check. This boy is inspecting his pet's coat and skin for mites. If this is done every day, a guinea pig should live a healthy life of five years or more.

Handling time gives you a chance to give your pets a quick health check. Run your fingers through the coat to see that there are no lice or other **parasites**. The eyes should be bright with no **discharge**, and the mouth and nose should be clean. About once a week check the front teeth for any damage. Look in the hutch for the guinea pigs' **droppings**, which should be hard and not runny.

Hygiene

Remember that you should always wash your hands before and after feeding or handling any pet. It is sometimes claimed that guinea pigs can catch colds from humans, so you may have to ask someone else to feed your pets if you have a cold or flu.

Guinea pigs must not be left without any attention for more than a day or two. If you go on vacation, you must have someone look after your pets for you. It should be someone your guinea pigs know, and who understands how to take care of them. It is a good idea to leave a note by the hutch with a reminder about giving greens and water.

Keeping everything clean

Guinea pigs are clean animals and like to live in clean surroundings. Apart from this, the cleanliness of the hutch will help to keep your pets in good health and prevent them from smelling. Dirty, smelly guinea pigs are not apt to be healthy or happy, and will not be popular pets.

The daily routine

Before feeding your pets, remove any left-over food and see if there is anything that they never eat. Look near the food bowl for any food that has been spilled, and remove it. Never add new food. Always empty the bowl and rinse it under the tap. Deal with the water bottle in the same manner, wipe the spout clean each day and make sure that it is not blocked.

See if any of the bedding has become wet, and replace it if it has. Finally, clean the "toilet" area with a small brush and scraper.

▼ The hutch should be cleaned out each week. While this is being done you can put your pets in the traveling box or in the outdoor run. Use a scraper to remove the droppings from the corners of the hutch.

▲ From time to time scrub the floor of the hutch using a mild disinfectant. If you choose a sunny day, you can then put the hutch outside in the sun to dry. Do not put in the new bedding until the floor of the hutch is completely dry.

The weekly routine

Once a week you should give the hutch a thorough cleaning. If you have a hutch with a sliding door between its two parts, you can shut your pets in one side while you clean the other. If not, you will need an escape-proof box to put them in.

Take out all the bedding and put it in the trash can or on a **compost** heap. Scrape any dirt off the floor of the hutch with a small shovel or paint scraper. Check the inside of the hutch for dangerous nails, splinters or rough edges of wire. When you have finished, put in clean, fresh bedding.

Now and then, you should scrub the floor of the hutch, using a mild **disinfectant**. Choose a fine day so that you can stand the hutch in the sun to dry. Do not use more water than necessary. The hutch must be completely dry before you put in fresh bedding. After all cleaning jobs, you should wash your hands.

Grooming

The appearance of a guinea pig's coat is a clue to its health. A healthy guinea pig will have a smooth, glossy coat. If your pet's coat looks dull, it may be a sign that you are not giving it the correct diet.

Guinea pigs normally **groom** themselves, using their front paws, to keep their coats in good condition.

Brushing the coat

If your guinea pigs are long-haired, they will need a daily brushing to avoid tangles. You should buy a soft baby brush and use it very gently. Most guinea pigs will enjoy being brushed and will stay still while you do it. Short-haired types need be brushed only once a week. Always brush in the direction in which the hair grows.

Unless you plan to put your guinea pigs in a show, it is best not to wash them as there is always a danger that they may catch a chill.

▼ Smooth-haired guinea pigs groom themselves using their front paws, but you should give their coats a gentle brushing once a week. Rough-haired and long-haired breeds should be groomed every day to avoid tangles and untidy coats.

Guinea pigs sometimes pick up small white lice from their hay. You may see lice moving in their coats as you brush them. They are quite harmless to guinea pigs and to humans, but they may make your pets uncomfortable. You can buy special sprays or powders from the pet shop to get rid of lice. Make sure that you know how to use them and always keep them away from an animal's eyes, nose and mouth.

Teeth and claws

If you provide a block of wood for your pets to gnaw, their teeth should stay in trim. If the front teeth, called the **incisors**, grow too long your pet will have difficulty eating. Trimming the teeth is a job for the vet. It is done quickly and is no more painful than when you cut your own fingernails.

You may also need to take your guinea pigs to the vet if their claws get too long. If you make a habit of inspecting your pets' claws once a week you will soon notice if the claws are getting too long.

▲ If you find lice or fleas in your pet's coat you can get dusting powder or a spray from the pet shop or vet. When using this, shield the guinea pig's eyes and face with one hand while spraying with the other hand. Wash your hands thoroughly afterward.

▶ This guinea pig has overgrown incisor teeth. Do not let your pet's teeth grow as long as these. Put a small log in the hutch for the animal to gnaw at. If this does not work, take your guinea pig to the vet who will be able to trim the incisors painlessly.

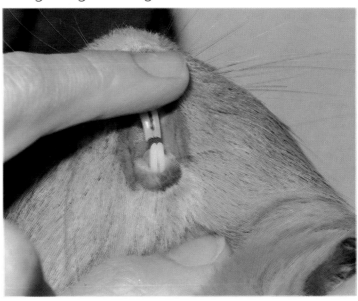

Health care

If you follow the advice in this book it will not be hard to provide your guinea pigs with a healthy **environment** that will keep them in good condition. You should make sure that the environment is as good as it can be, and keep an eye open for possible health problems.

Preventing illness

Damp, drafts and overheating are all dangers to good health. Always make sure that all bedding is dry and take any damp material away. The position of the hutch or run is very important. If it is outside, it must be weatherproof and away from drafts and direct sunlight. Guinea pigs suffer if there is too much heat, and they should always be able to find a shady spot to rest in.

Be careful to remove any stale food which could cause health problems, and make sure that your pets have enough vitamin C in their diet. In winter, when it can be difficult to find wild greens, you can feed them lettuce leaves and bits of fruit and vegetables.

▶ This photo shows a guinea pig with a mite beneath its coat. If you stroke your pet the wrong way, from tail to head, you will be able to see if your pet is infected with mites. They look like tiny white flakes. The pet shop may be able to advise you how to get rid of this pest.

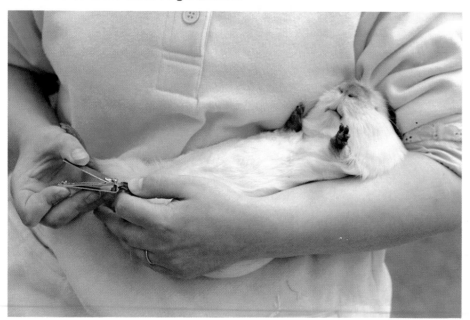

◀ In the wild, a guinea pig is able to wear down its claws by constant movement. If your pet's claws grow too long, you can buy nail clippers from the pet shop. Do not clip too close to the base of the nail.

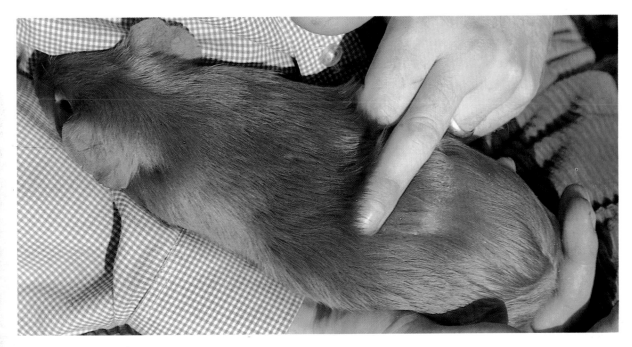

Signs and symptoms

A healthy guinea pig is active by day, either eating or playing. Lack of activity is often a sign of ill health. Sick guinea pigs eat little. There may be wetness about the eyes or nose.

Itching can cause guinea pigs so much **stress** that they die. If your pet seems to scratch its coat more than usual you should take it to the vet.

Diarrhea can be caused by eating too many greens. Feed only mash or pellets if diarrhea occurs, but ask a vet's advice if the problem does not clear up in a day or two.

Chills in guinea pigs can lead to **pneumonia**, which is serious. The signs of pneumonia are wheezy breathing and shivering. You should take your pet to the vet as soon as possible.

Guinea pigs that have become overheated should be moved to a cool but dry and draft-free place until they have recovered.

A sick guinea pig should always be housed alone until it is completely well again.

▼ If the hay is dusty your guinea pig may get dirty ears. You can use a cotton swab, slightly moistened with warm water, to clean the outer ear.

Varieties of coats

Most of the guinea pigs you see in pet shops are not **purebred**. Their parents and grandparents may have had different varieties of coats and colors. This does not matter unless you want to breed or show them. Provided they are healthy, "**mongrel**" guinea pigs make excellent pets.

Guinea pig breeders recognize about 25 purebred types, which vary in color or type of coat. New varieties are being added as more breeders develop them. Although you will be happy keeping smooth-haired "mongrels," it is interesting to see other types. A local breeder will often be glad to show you around, and you should visit any local shows. Guinea pigs have three different types of coats:

Smooth-haired

Smooth-haired guinea pigs are sometimes called English, American or Bolivian, but these are all different names for the same type. It has a smooth, glossy coat which may be **self-colored**, meaning that it is the same color all over, or may have markings of different colors.

▼ The picture shows a fine pair of smooth-haired guinea pigs. On the left is a Golden Agouti, and on the right a Beige Satin.

In the wild, all guinea pigs are smooth-haired. Most guinea pigs from pet shops are smooth-haired and these are the easiest to groom.

Rough-haired

Another name for the rough-haired type is the Abyssinian. Its coat grows from a number of different centers, which are called **rosettes**, and it has a ridge along its spine. The hair is about 4 cm (1.5 in) long and is coarse to the touch.

Long-haired

The long-haired type, sometimes called the Peruvian, has long, soft hair which needs a great deal of attention every day to keep it clean and tidy. For this reason, the long-haired guinea pig is not a good choice as a pet. It is really a guinea pig for the expert who will want to **exhibit** it at shows.

The Silky or Sheltie is another long-haired type. It is similar to the Peruvian, but has no fringe of hair on its head.

▲ The rough-haired Tortoiseshell-and-White (or Tortie) is a favorite pet, but this breed needs a daily grooming if the coat is to remain in good condition.

▼ The soft and silky coat of the Long-haired Peruvian guinea pig hangs down to the ground and may even cover the head and face. These animals are favored for showing, but are not good as first pets since they need so much attention every day.

Color varieties

One reason why guinea pigs are such popular pets is the fact that their coats are colorful and varied. Before making your final choice, it is a good idea to learn the different colors. The coat of the wild guinea pig is a speckled gray color all over. This color is called **agouti**. All today's color varieties have been bred from agoutis. Breeders have taken guinea pigs with slight differences in color and mated them to produce new color varieties. This is called **selective breeding**.

The markings for the different color varieties are laid down in **standards** published by national guinea pig breeders' clubs. If you have bought purebred guinea pigs and are interested in breeding from them for show, you will have to obtain a copy of the standard for your variety.

▼ Self-colored guinea pigs, known as "selfs," have coats of one overall color. In this picture, you can see six different color varieties. From left to right these are Black, Pink-eyed Golden, Dark-eyed Golden, Lilac, Pink-eyed White and Chocolate.

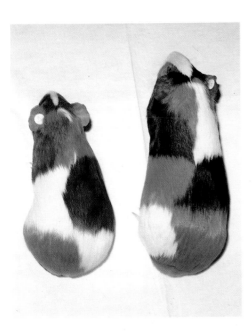

▲ There are also patterned varieties that have coats of two or three colors. Seen from above, these Tricolored Tortoiseshell-and-White guinea pigs show how their different colors are sharply separated into panels of roughly equal size.

Self-colored

Selfs are smooth-coated guinea pigs with one overall color. Most breeders recognize eight colors. They are black, white, cream, golden, red, chocolate, beige and lilac. In the United States, there is also a blue variety.

Agoutis

Agouti varieties have no pattern on their smooth coats, but their hair varies in color from the base, where it enters the skin, to the tip. This gives them a speckled appearance which is called "**ticking**." There are six agouti varieties — golden, silver, cinnamon, salmon, chocolate and lemon.

Marked varieties

Marked, or patterned, guinea pigs have two or three colors in their coats. The pattern you are most likely to see is the Dutch, which is white with a colored rump and face markings. The band of white around the front of the guinea pig's body is called the saddle. The second color can be orange-red, black, chocolate, agouti, yellow or cream.

The Himalayan is all white except for colored "points" on the nose, ears and feet. The points may be black or chocolate.

The Tortoiseshell or "Tortie" is difficult to breed and so is not often seen. It has patches of black, red and white which should be of equal size with perfectly straight edges between them.

Rough-coat and long-hair colors

With rough-coated and long-haired varieties it is the condition of the coat, not the color, that is important at a show. The guinea pigs can be any color or combination of colors.

Showing guinea pigs

Exhibiting guinea pigs at shows is an interesting and exciting hobby, but you will have to spend much time training and preparing your pets for the show. The best way to find out about showing is to join a local club if there is one in your area. Remember that if you enter your pets in a show they will be competing against guinea pigs whose owners may have spent years learning how to exhibit animals in top condition.

Even if you do not exhibit your own guinea pigs, it is interesting to find out more about showing. This will help you to get more fun out of your own pets.

▲ Imagine the noise at this show with all the guinea pigs squeaking! In Britain, the National Cavy Club lays down the rules and standards by which guinea pigs are judged. In the United States, it is the American Cavy Breeders Association. In addition to national shows, there are also local shows with pet classes for beginners.

Rules and classes

Every show has a set of rules that exhibitors must follow. If you are interested in a show, get a copy of the rules and read it carefully. You may find that there are different classes for young and **mature** guinea pigs, and for boars and sows, as well as for the different coat and color varieties.

▲ This long-haired Sheltie guinea pig is being brushed gently with a baby's soft hair brush before the show.

Showing your pet

Even if you do not want to try one of the big shows for guinea pigs, you may have a chance to show your guinea pigs at a local pet show where different small pets are exhibited. If you exhibit at any kind of show, your guinea pigs must be used to being handled, as the judges will want to inspect them closely.

You will need a clean, escape-proof and well-ventilated box in which to take your pet to the show. When you arrive, an official may put a sticky label behind the animal's ear and tell you where to put your guinea pig. At some shows one of the officials may take your pet to the judges' table to be examined and then return it to you afterward.

The judges will be looking for clean, well-groomed and well-fed animals. Never take a sick animal to a show. The judges will refuse to see it, and it may spread disease among the other entries.

▶ A Coronet and a Sheltie guinea pig are being examined by the show judge. The Coronet is like a Sheltie, but has a crest on its head.

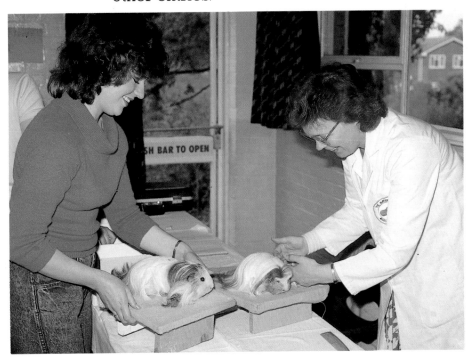

Breeding guinea pigs

If you wish to breed guinea pigs you will have to be able to tell male from female. The illustration may help you, but if you are in doubt ask the vet or someone at the pet shop to sex your guinea pigs for you.

Boars and sows should not be brought together for mating before they are six months old, and some breeders prefer to leave the first mating until eight months. Do not start breeding unless you know of good homes for up to four young guinea pigs.

Mating

You will not need any special equipment except a spare hutch for the boar when the birth is due. Guinea pigs do not always mate quickly. You may have to be patient after you have put the boar and sow together. One boar may be put with two or more sows.

Each sow can be mated for only a few hours every 18 days. So you will need to keep boar and sows together for 36 days to give them a chance of mating. The best seasons for successful mating are spring and summer.

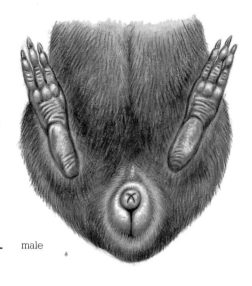

male

▼ This picture shows a breeding boar (center) and two sows. As guinea pigs do not always mate quickly, you may put a boar with two or more sows to be sure of a successful mating.

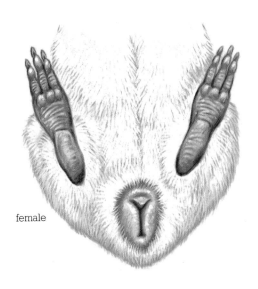

female

▲ It soon becomes obvious when a sow becomes pregnant by the size of her stomach. At this point she should be moved to a hutch of her own with a nesting box and plenty of hay.

Pregnancy

The boar and sow can stay together after they have mated, but the boar should be separated from the sow when the birth is due. The reason for this is that the boar may try to mate again after the birth, and might injure the young in the process.

The **gestation period** — the time from mating to birth — is between nine and ten weeks. Once you think the sow may be pregnant, do not handle her or you may damage the young ones. An early sign of pregnancy is that she will start to eat more, and at five or six weeks she will begin to look heavier as the young grow inside her.

Pregnant sows need extra food, and extra supplies of greens for vitamin C. Bread soaked in milk makes good extra food for a pregnant sow. She will drink more water than usual, so you must make sure that the water bottle is kept full.

The young family

Sows do not build nests for their young. There are usually between two and four young in a **litter**. They are born with fur, are able to see and their teeth are already formed.

The newborn litter

Guinea pigs give birth easily, and the sow will lick her young clean and will clear up the mess from the birth. The newly born young will suck their mother's milk and cuddle close to her to keep warm. In an hour or so after birth they may start to move about and may even try nibbling a little dry food.

It is very tempting to bring your family and friends to see the newborn guinea pigs, but you should keep other people away for the first few days so that the young are not frightened.

Your job is to make sure that the birth has gone well and that there are no dead cubs or sickly ones that the mother is not looking after.

▼ A litter of young guinea pigs is great fun for the owner. The average litter size is three or four, the young being born fully developed and able to move around. They begin to eat solid food after a day or two, and are suckled for only about two weeks.

▲ Although only a few days old, these young guinea pigs are able to enjoy nibbling grass in an outdoor run.

▼ They soon learn to nibble cabbage leaves as their teeth are already cut and growing.

Sometimes a sow may push away a cub when it tries to snuggle up, if there is something wrong with it. You should remove the sickly cub and ask the vet to put it down. It has no chance of living if it is unable to nurse properly.

Growing up

The young will continue to take milk from the sow until they are about three or four weeks old. During this time she must have three meals a day, with plenty of greens and bread soaked in milk. She will teach her young to eat by taking pieces of food to them, and gradually they will want less of her milk. From this time on the young guinea pigs will begin to grow very quickly.

Before the young are four weeks old you must separate the boars from the sows to prevent them from mating. You should also keep an eye on the boars, which should be separated if they start to fight. After about six weeks the young can go to their new owners.

Glossary

agouti: the natural color of wild guinea pigs

boar: a fully-grown male guinea pig

burrow: (1) a hole in the ground made by an animal as its home. (2) to dig a hole

cavy: the other name for a guinea pig

chemical: a substance that may be harmful to animals. Chemicals are often used on the land to kill weeds and to make plants grow well

closed: lying smooth and flat

cobby: describes an animal that has a solid and firm body

colony: a group of animals living together

compost: dead vegetable matter left to rot

diarrhea: a stomach upset that causes loose or runny droppings

diet: the types of food usually eaten by an animal

digest: to turn food into energy

discharge: runny matter coming from the eyes, ears or nose

disinfectant: a chemical that kills germs

droppings: solid waste matter from the body

environment: the surroundings in which an animal lives

exercise: the use of body muscles by walking, running or climbing

exhibit: to put on show

fragile: easily broken

gestation period: the length of time between mating and giving birth

groom: to clean and tidy the coat

incisor: a sharp, chisel-like tooth at the front of the mouth used for gnawing

instinct: natural behavior, which does not have to be learned

litter: (1) the young guinea pigs resulting from one mating. (2) the material used to cover the floor of a cage

mature: fully grown

mongrel: an animal with parents each of different color or coat varieties

parasite: an insect found in a guinea pig's coat

pellet: food mixed together into a small, hard ball

pneumonia: a disease of the lungs causing difficulty in breathing

pollute: to poison the environment

pregnant: describes a female when young are growing inside her body

purebred: having been bred from parents of the same color or coat variety

rodent: an animal that gnaws and nibbles with its front teeth

rosette: an arrangement of hair which sprouts from the center like a cowlick

rump: the hindquarters of an animal

selective breeding: breeding from a carefully selected male and female to produce young with required looks and qualities

self-colored: the same color all over the body

sow: a fully-grown female guinea pig

species: a group of similar animals

standard: the rules laid down for judging guinea pigs of particular coat or color varieties

stress: nervous illness in which an animal becomes very anxious

ticking: speckles

vegetarian: an animal that eats only vegetable food

vitamin C: a substance found in certain foods in small amounts. It is needed for good health

Further reading

Leda Blumberg, *Pets*, Franklin Watts, 1983
Fiona Henrie, *Guinea Pigs*, Franklin Watts, 1981
Joyce Pope, *Taking Care of Your Guinea Pig*, Franklin Watts, 1986

Useful addresses

American Humane Association, P.O. Box 1226, Denver, Colorado 80201
American Society for the Prevention of Cruelty to Animals, 441 East 92nd Street,
  New York, NY 10028
The Humane Society of the United States, 2100 L Street, NW, Washington, DC 20037

Index